This book is dedicated to my almost sister-in-law,
who insisted I do something with my zany chalkboard drawings.
"A book," she said.

It's hard to say no to Nan.

D1283609

WHAT'S ON THE BOARD?

Menus and recipes inspired by,
and illustrated for, my very special friends.
They have interesting stories,
that's why they're invited for dinner.

NEIL FOX

PREFACE

Fifteen or so years ago, while rummaging through a dusty junk shop, I found an old wood-framed tabletop chalkboard. It was like the chalkboards bistros use to display the daily specials.

I bought it.

Since then, when we invite friends for dinner my chalkboard displays the night's menu, illustrating the ingredients and something about the friends I love cooking for.

What's on the board?

That's usually what friends ask when they're invited to dinner.

My chalkboard has magical qualities. It provides more than the expected answer, it conveys the importance of our friendship, what it means to me. It telegraphs the wonderful evening ahead. The delectable meal we'll share. A meal that will satisfy stomach and heart. My guest's and my own.

From a tugboat captain, to the heir to a herring empire, my friends are an interesting mix. How our lives intertwined would make a delightful Wes Anderson movie.

This book brings together friends, their stories, memories of meals shared, pieces of my history. In effect, *What's on the Board?* is a bit of a memoir, perhaps a love story.

However, keeping in mind that this is a cookbook, each story comes with an easy-to-recreate delicious dish that will bring a smile to your lips and a tingle to your palette.

A NOTE ON RECIPES

For me, cooking is a creative endeavor equal to painting, composing a song, writing a story, penning a poem. Ingredients and measures are meant to be directional, to inspire. Feel free to add a bit more salt, an extra clove of garlic, your favorite spice or herb. That said, I hope the cookbook authors who have inspired a recipe here will be OK with my transgressions.

I give original names to many of the dishes I make, symptomatic of an old advertising guy who loves branding.

As you start producing a recipe, get in the mood. Put on a favorite music selection, (for me it's Aretha, Mongo Santamaria, Al Green, Maria Callas), turn the volume up, pour yourself a glass of wine, and start cooking.

A last note. All recipes serve four, unless indicated.

CONTENTS

Friends, Chalkboards, Stories and Recipes

FRIENDS, CHALKBOARDS, STORIES AND RECIPES

FASHION FORWARD AT 92

RUTHIE WAS Dad's third wife. Twenty years his junior, he met her in a Buffalo supermarket. She was the owner's niece. Dad was calling on her uncle, selling him salami and cheese specialties. That's what Dad did after he retired, he sold cold cuts to food stores.

Now widowed from his second wife, hardly finished mourning the passing of wife #2, he was immediately smitten with Ruthie, and so was Ruthie smitten with Dad. They married. Over the next twenty plus years, they lived a love story, until Dad passed in his eighties.

I remember Ruthie and Dad visiting us shortly after their marriage. We were living in Chicago at the time. We picked them up at O'Hare. Ruthie had something tucked under her coat. "What's that?" Turned out it was a kitten just weeks old, a surprise gift she thought the kids would love. She was right, and eventually we loved the kitten too. We named her Star.

It was apparent from our first meeting Ruthie was Auntie Mame incarnate. An optimistic, self-directed, stylish woman—to this day, fashion forward. Now, 92 years old, Ruthie remains optimistic, caring, always reminiscing about Dad.

"I know Sid's looking after us. I loved your dad. Everybody did."

And we love Ruthie. Everyone does. And when she visits next, she gets my daughter Mindy's recipe for Chicken Noodle Soup with leeks, peas and dill.* We all love that too.

---

* From Mindy Fox's *A Bird in the Oven and Then Some*.
https://www.amazon.com/Bird-Oven-Then-Some-Delectable/product-reviews/1906868336

ROAST CHICKEN NOODLE SOUP WITH LEEKS, PEAS AND DILL

Nothing will thrill Ruthie more than having a bowl of chicken noodle soup, from Mindy's cookbook, *A Bird in the Oven and Then Some.*

INGREDIENTS

- 2 tablespoons olive oil
- 3 leeks, sliced lengthwise and thoroughly washed. Tough outer leaves removed, white and very pale parts cut crosswise into $\frac{1}{3}$ inch pieces

  Flakey coarse salt

  Freshly ground black pepper
- 7 cups chicken broth, preferably homemade
- 1 garlic clove, smashed and peeled
- 1$\frac{1}{4}$ cup thin noodles
- 3 cups roasted chicken, shredded
- 2 cups frozen peas, thawed
- 2 tablespoons finely chopped dill

PREP

Heat oil in large skillet over medium heat. Add the leeks in a single layer, cut side down.

Reduce flame to medium-low.

Season leeks with generous pinches of salt and pepper, turning once, reduce heat, repeat until both sides are golden brown.

Meanwhile, bring the broth and garlic to a boil in a 5-quart pot.

Stir in the noodles, cook until tender, about 10-12 minutes. Remove from heat, discard garlic.

Set aside a few leeks per serving for garnish. Add the remaining leeks to the soup, along with chicken, peas, and dill. Cook 2 minutes more.

Season with salt and pepper. Ladle into bowls and garnish with the reserved leeks.

SAM

THE CREATIVE GUY

BACK IN the day, we shared a love for coming up with great advertising ideas for clients like M&M/Mars, Colgate, and Lego.

There're plenty of stories about Sam I could tell. Here's just one.

Among the projects we worked on was a new business venture we launched for ourselves.

We bought the exclusive licensing rights to the entire bank of *The New Yorker* cartoons for internet advertising.

Our concept, offer big brands category-specific cartoons and an ad message. For Hilton (travel), Chivas Regal (drinking), AARP (seniors), sending their customers a laugh along with a selling message.

Sam anointed our new advertising venture Punchline. Everyone thought it was a brilliant idea. But, despite our best efforts, we couldn't sell enough cartoons to guarantee retirement on a tropical island, with Sam relaxing in a hammock after a hard day on the golf course.

After two years we celebrated the closing of Punchline with a dinner of my much loved Codfish Veracruz, along with a bottle of six-month-old vinho verde. By the way, Sam's from Kansas, where Codfish Veracruz rarely appears on the menu.

CODFISH VERACRUZ

The great thing about cod is that it can be prepared in a myriad of ways. This recipe emboldens the fish with the spicy flavor of chorizo, a few hand-picked spices and the salty taste of the clams, all presented beautifully on the pan the cod is cooked in, then sprinkled with a finishing touch of parsley.

INGREDIENTS

20	Littleneck clams, thoroughly scrubbed, then allowed to sit for two hours in water, with 2 tablespoons white wine vinegar
1½	lb center-cut cod loin
8"	of chorizo cut into ¼ inch rounds
¼	cup olive oil
⅓	cup warmed white wine
1	Poblano pepper, seeded, sliced lengthwise into strips
1	medium onion, roughly diced
4	large cloves garlic, medium diced
½	teaspoon Aleppo pepper flakes
¼	teaspoon paprika
1	teaspoon flaky sea salt, such as Maldon
4	good grinds of black pepper
¼	cup flat leaf parsley, diced
1	baguette

Pre-heat oven to 400°.

In a large pan heat oil on low flame, add chorizo, poblano pepper, onion, garlic.

When onion turns translucent, about 5 minutes, increase flame to medium. Add white wine.

Continue cooking 2 minutes, add clams. Cover pan. Cook for additional 8-10 minutes until clams open. Discard those that didn't open.

Remove remaining clams and set aside.

Sprinkle both sides of cod with flakey salt, fresh ground pepper, paprika and Aleppo pepper.

Add cod to pan turning fish to get both sides thoroughly coated with pan mixture.

Transfer pan to oven, leave uncovered.

Bake fish 8 minutes, then turn oven to broil . Cook for an additional 3 minutes. Fish should be lightly crisped.

Remove from oven, add back clams.

Spoon pan juices and their ingredients liberally over clams and fish.

Serve in bowls with a sprinkling of parsley and slices of crusty baguette.

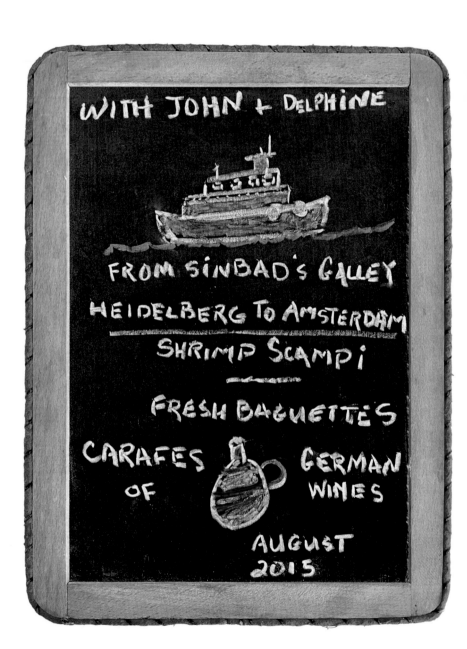

WITH JOHN + DELPHINE

FROM SINBAD'S GALLEY

HEIDELBERG TO AMSTERDAM

SHRIMP SCAMPI

FRESH BAGUETTES

CARAFES OF GERMAN WINES

AUGUST 2015

THE VOYAGE ABOARD SINBAD

I MET JOHN in London in the mid-60's. We were young, energetic ad guys working for a fast-growing British based ad agency. We became friends. A half century later, living on opposite sides of the Atlantic (we hadn't been in touch for several years) up popped a message from John inviting me to join him and Delphine, his wife, on a voyage through the Baltics aboard their new tugboat, Sinbad.

A month later we met on a dock in Heidelberg, where Sinbad was moored. For 10 days we motored through the locks of the Neckar River eating delicious food, sampling German wine, and telling stories. Lots of stories. Here's one John shared.

John was a boy of three in 1939 when Hitler invaded England. A year later, the Blitzkrieg started.

John's dad was headmaster of the Dartmouth Royal Naval College, Britain's equivalent to America's Annapolis. The College was a bombing target for the German Luftwaffe.

The day machine-gunning started and the shells began to fall, in a daylight attack, John's father was hosting a lunchtime meeting of British admirals and assorted bigwigs. The memory John took away is of the grown-ups terrified and huddling in the kitchen corridor.

John saw the adults he looked up to lose their nerve, unable to come up with a plan. It stayed with him. John survived and grew stronger as a result of the experience.

John and Delphine met while competing in sailing events—she often bested him. Their shared love of the sea and sailing resulted in my assignment as Sinbad's cook. They loved my Shrimp Scampi.

SHRIMP SCAMPI

We found a fish monger in Heidelberg with the most wonderful collection of sea creatures. The shrimp, big and succulent, came with the fragrance of the sea. Accompanied by a properly chilled Riesling Spätlese Trocken, our first dinner at sea in their tugboat was a most civilized affair.

INGREDIENTS

24	medium-large wild caught shrimp
6	garlic cloves minced
¼	cup bread crumbs
1	tablespoon oregano
2	tablespoons virgin olive oil
	Salt
1	teaspoon red pepper flakes
½	cup dry white wine, such as Pinot Grigio
	Several good grinds of black pepper
	Juice of ½ lemon
1	fresh baguette split lengthwise, sliced into 3" pieces
½	cup parsley, finely chopped

PREP

Slice open back of shrimp deep enough to expose vein. Remove vein, careful not to dislodge shell.

Butterfly shrimp by pressing opened area lightly against cutting board.

Transfer shrimp to plastic bag. Add olive oil, salt, pepper flakes, freshly ground black pepper, oregano, garlic, bread crumbs. Shake thoroughly.

In a large skillet, heat oil.

Add shrimp and mixture, 6-8 shrimp at a time depending on skillet size (don't crowd). Cook on medium heat, until shrimps turn pink and bread crumbs brown, about 4 minutes.

Set shrimp aside on paper towel to drain excess oil.

Add the dry white wine to the pan. Increase flame until wine reduces by half. Just a few minutes.

Plate shrimp, cover with wine and pan drippings. Add chopped parsley.

Serve with slices of baguette to mop up any remaining garlic and drippings.

Note: Keeping shell on shrimp while cooking adds the flavor of the sea. The place from whence they came.

THE RENAISSANCE MAN AND THE KING

MASSIMO, ARRIVED from Rome as a teenager with a troupe of his fellow actors in the 70's. Photos showing Massimo of his time back then reminded me of scenes from a Fellini movie.

Massimo fell in love with New York. He came back a year later deciding this was his home. So why have I dubbed him Renaissance man? Because he is an actor, storyteller, filmmaker, playwright, director, and founder of Printsource, a successful fabric design exhibit company.

I met Massimo through James King, who I refer to as The King. James does have a royal way about him.

James and I started out as work colleagues, when I consulted for Harlem Stage, helping with branding and marketing. James, their general manager, supervised staff, union operations, executing artists contracts, etc. etc. etc.

We shared an office which had its ups and downs. Mostly ups, until I left and James ultimately moved on to become the Creative Director of the PBS WNET All Arts channel: a great job that won him and Channel 13 several Emmys.

Ellen and I, James and Massimo, we're a quartet. We travel together, hang out in New York. They visit us in the Berkshires for hikes, museum visits, shopping, especially for shoes at the Cole Hann outlet. James is competing with Imelda Marcos in that regard.

And then, there's food and cooking their favorite grilled Berkshire pork sausage.

BERKSHIRE SAUSAGE, GRILLED GARLIC, BLISTERED PEPPERS AND ONION

This is one of my favorites, an ultra-easy summertime dish. We're lucky to live in the Berks, where there is access to farm-raised beef, pork and chicken. That said, wherever you live, always ask where the meat you're buying was raised and support local sourcing.

INGREDIENTS

4-6	pork sausages, hot or sweet or a combination
2	large onions roughly chopped
2	bell peppers (one red and one yellow), seeds and membranes removed, sliced in strips
4	whole garlic bulbs, tops removed
¼	cup olive oil
1	baguette

PREP

Pre-heat grill to 400°.

Rinse sausages then thoroughly dry with paper towels.

Add sausages to grill, close grill cover. Turn sausages after 3 minutes, grill for 3 minutes more.

Add peppers and onions, continue grilling 3-4 minutes, cover down until peppers blister and onion begins to brown.

Ready! Transfer sausage, onion and pepper to serving platter along with slices of crispy baguette.

"DO I DARE EAT A PEACH?"

MARSHA AND JAY, Jay and Marsha, always a twosome until we lost Jay eight years ago. I think of Jay often and let loose a tear or two when I remember a New Year's Eve party at their place.

Jay and I decided we'd entertain the girls with a poetry reading. We both enjoy T.S. Eliot's *The Love Song of J. Alfred Prufrock*.

Themes of love, identity, aging, self. I can hear our voices, our laughter.

"In the room the women come and go
Talking of Michelangelo....
I grow old... I grow old...
I shall wear the bottoms of my trousers rolled....
I have heard the mermaids singing, each to each.
I do not think they will sing to me....
Shall I part my hair behind? Do I dare eat a peach?"

Now it's Ellen and Marsha and me. We have dinner, the three of us, as often as possible. We've branded our evenings The Supper Club. One of Marsha's favorite dishes is Clams Posillipo.

If Jay was still with us at the table, he might glance at Marsha and add another line of *Prufrock's*:

"Is it perfume from a dress
That makes me so digress?"

Marsha's of course.

CLAMS POSILLIPO
OR SPAGHETTI ALLE VONGOLE

I love clams, prepared any way. Made this way satisfies my hunger for succulent clams and for pasta al dente.

INGREDIENTS

3	pounds manila clams thoroughly scrubbed, rinsed and left to sit in cold water with 2 tablespoons of white vinegar for an hour
⅓	cup olive oil, plus a tablespoon or two for mixing with cooked pasta
6	large cloves garlic, minced
½	cup white wine, Pinot Grigio will do
1	teaspoon sea salt
4	good grinds black pepper
½	teaspoon Aleppo pepper
1	tablespoon oregano
2	tablespoons parsley, chopped
¾	lb. De Cecco #12 spaghetti

Start with pasta.

Fill large pot with water (about ¾ full). Add 1 tablespoon salt. Bring salted water to boil, before adding pasta. Cook pasta at a steady boil for 10 minutes.

Taste a strand. Texture should be al dente, slightly undercooked, not too firm and not too soft.

Drain pasta, setting aside ¼ cup pasta water. Transfer pasta to large bowl, sprinkle with olive oil to keep the pasta moist until ready to add clams.

While pasta is cooking, prepare clams.

In a sauté pan large enough to hold spaghetti and clams, warm olive oil. Add garlic, continue cooking at low temp, about 1 minute.

Add salt, pepper, Aleppo, continue cooking another minute.

Add white wine, increase flame to medium. Cook, stirring, until liquid is reduced by half.

Turn up heat slightly, add clams, cover pan, continue cooking until clams open, about 7 minutes. (If a clam does not open, discard it.)

Add pasta to clams and broth, mix well, careful not to loosen clams from their shell. Add oregano. Continue cooking for an additional 2 minutes.

Add an ounce or two of reserved pasta water if sauce requires.

Sprinkle with chopped parsley and serve.

FROM SANTA MONICA
CALIFORNIA
MATT BRYANT
WELCOME!

SWORDFISH!

ORANGE
LIME
LEMON
GRILLED WITH SLICES OR:
CORN ON THE COBB
GRAPE FRUIT
SUMMER SALAD
PLUS!
"JEANIE + BARRIE"

A LIFE SAVER

MATT, AN ENGLISHMAN, came to the US in his 20's, ultimately launching a very successful media buying company. Being in the same industry we came to know one another and became friends.

At the time I served on the board of Outward Bound. I invited Matt to join me on a rafting trip down the Green River in Utah, a fundraising event.

One of the trip's activities included an exercise in teamwork. There were 18 participants, almost all CEO's here in the wilderness. Each of us were to swim to an outcropping in the middle of a very fast section of the river. Then wait until every man stood on the rock together. The only equipment offered was one life preserver tethered to a forty-foot length of rope.

When the instructor gave the go-ahead, all of us jumped in the raging current, frantically trying to reach the rock. No one made it.

Now back on shore, soaking wet, we realized this was an exercise in teamwork and came up with a plan. The strongest swimmer would cross the river first, rope and life preserver in hand, then toss the life preserver back to land as an assist for the next man. I was the last to cross. I remember Matt's encouragement and all the strength it took as I struggled to reach the rock. Matt was there, arm outstretched—my life saver.

Matt joined me again on an initiative helping raise money for City Harvest's efforts to feed 9/11 first responders. Matt's influence with the media gained millions of dollars in free print and broadcast ads created to raise funds. He's a life saver again. He deserves my tropical approach to grilling swordfish.

SUMMER SWORDFISH

I call this dish Summer Swordfish because of the lemon, orange, and lime slices that are grilled alongside it. A very simple recipe that will tingle your taste buds.

An important note about cooking fish, whether grilling, baking or frying: Never overcook. My rule of thumb 7 minutes, 3.5 minutes/side, for almost all fish whether grilled, broiled or fried. (Baked fish may take a bit longer, about 10 minutes.) Remember, you can always put back fish to cook a minute more, but there's no turning back for fish that is overcooked, dried out.

INGREDIENTS

2	lbs slice of swordfish
2	cloves garlic, minced
¼	cup soy sauce
¼	cup olive oil
1	tablespoon kosher salt
4	good grinds of black pepper
1	orange, 1 lime, 1 lemon, each cut in half-inch rounds

PREP

Salt swordfish on both sides, follow with grinds of pepper.

Spread minced garlic on both sides of fish.

Add soy sauce and oil to create marinade. Marinate in refrigerator for an hour or two.

Heat grill to 400°. Add fruit slices, grill one minute per side. Put fruit aside.

Grill fish 3.5 minutes per side.

Plate fish along with fruit, instructing guests to squeeze their choice of fruit over fish.

Serve with corn on the cob and a green salad.

WELOME LUCY, SCOUT
DODGER, JON + BRAD
"YOU NEED TO BE FED"
SO: A LITTLE BREAKFAST OF
SMOKED SALMON W DILL +CC
COFFEE OR TEA

THEN FOR LUNCH:
GUACAMOLE + CHIPS
WHITE SHAKSHUKA
LOCAL TOMATO + SPROUTS + GREENS
BERSHIRE CHABATTA

ROASTED PEACHES + YOGURT
POUCHED PEARS + YOGURT

CHOICE OF BEVERAGE

FROM HERRING TO HONEY BEES

TALK ABOUT HERRING, just ask Jon, whose family put herring in a jar with vinegar (or cream sauce) and chopped onion.

Presto! Vita Herring was born.

I've so enjoyed hearing Jon tell stories about his father and uncle (brothers) who met and married two sisters whose family founded Vita Herring, a generation earlier.

My memories of Vita Herring in cream sauce start with accompanying my dad to buy bagels, bialys, lox and herring at our neighborhood appetizing store on Sunday mornings.

Of course, there's a lot more about Jon than herring. Jon is a chef. He came to NY from Seattle, started a very successful catering company, joined the Board of *God's Love We Deliver*, then co-conceived and created the *God's Love We Deliver Cookbook* with stories and recipes from 75 celebrity supporters.

I met Jon through Brad, his life partner, his husband. Brad and I go back to Harlem Stage (HS) where he was Program Director and I, his *marketing nemesis*. The 15-year consulting gig at HS was one of my most gratifying projects. Brad made it so, as he executed the HS mission to support the work of gifted artists of color.

So where do the bees come in? That's mostly Brad's responsibility. Brad takes care of the hives at their magical home in Sag Harbor. It's a place of spiritual delight that only Jon and Brad could have conceived.

While Jon doesn't stock jars of Vita in his pantry, Ellen and I are always happy to be gifted with a wonderful jar of honey whenever we visit these very special friends.

They visit us each fall, their annual Berkshire sojourn. This time they brought their 3 pooches. We cooked up poached eggs Shakshuka and local greens. It went well with a bottle of Albariño.

WHITE PEPPER SHAKSHUKA

White pepper has a more complex flavor than its brother black pepper. It adds an earthy taste, another dimension, to one of my favorite brunch dishes, Shakshuka.

INGREDIENTS

2 tablespoons olive oil

1 tablespoons harissa

2 teaspoons tomato paste

1 large red bell pepper, seeded and cut in thin lengthwise slices

4 cloves garlic, diced

1 teaspoon cumin

1 14 oz. can peeled tomatoes, Muir Glen or Centos are my favorites

4 large free-range eggs

½ cup sheep's yogurt (optional) or ½ cup sour cream (optional)

½ cup cilantro, chopped

1 teaspoon salt

½ teaspoon white pepper

PREP

Heat olive oil in large frying pan over medium heat.

Add harissa, tomato paste, peppers, garlic, cumin, cilantro, salt and white pepper.

Stir and cook for 7 minutes, sufficient to allow peppers to soften.

Add tomatoes, bring to simmer, cook for an additional 10 minutes or until sauce thickens.

Taste, adjust seasonings as needed.

Make 4 little impressions in the sauce, sufficient to hold a single egg bullseye. (You can use a small juice glass to mark the bullseye.)

Taking care, crack each egg into a bullseye. Try not to break yolks.

Cover frying pan and cook on low flame for 3½ minutes until yolks are set—runny is good. Remove from stove, allow eggs to settle.

Spoon one egg with sauce onto individual plates and serve with dollop of yogurt or sour cream on the side if desired. Sprinkle with additional cilantro.

THE ARTIST AMONG ARTISTS

WHAT DO Phillip Johnson, Stanley Tigerman, Robert Venturi, Denise Scott Brown, Robert Stern, Michael Graves, Charles Gwathmey, Robert Siegel, Richard Meier, Steven Holl and Ettore Scottass all have in common?

Aside from the fact that they are all masters of 21st century design, none of them could say no to Nan.

Nan, a gifted artist and designer in her own right, founded Swid Powell with her partner, Addie. They convinced these monarchs of modern design to individually create tabletop merchandise that would add their artistry to the presentation of food.

Now more than a quarter century later the Swid Powell Collection is a feature at the oldest college art museum in America, Yale University's Art Gallery.

Nan interprets her own art through encaustics, an ancient technique in which pigments are mixed with hot liquid wax, a burning-in of colors that is an essential element of the technique. Nan's work is extraordinary.

But crazy as it may seem, she loves my zany chalkboard menus. So, in addition to dedicating this book to her, here is her favorite Asian noodle salad, dubbed Open Sesame Noodle Salad.

As the intro to this book says, I too can't say no to Nan.

NAN'S OPEN SESAME NOODLE SALAD

There are unlimited ways to make Asian noodle salad. Give this recipe a try, then let loose your imagination on variations of your own making.

INGREDIENTS

1 lb	soba noodles (I like the buckwheat or brown rice varieties)
3	tablespoons good olive oil
1	tablespoon soy sauce
2	tablespoons rice vinegar
3	chopped scallions, green stems included
½	teaspoon Aleppo pepper
½	teaspoon Ubra Biber pepper available by mail from Kalustyan in NYC, or other good spice stores
3	garlic cloves, diced
½	cup cilantro, chopped

In medium sized pot, bring 5 cups of water to boil.

Add soba noodles, cook 7-10 minutes or as specified on package.

In a pan, warm olive oil on a low flame, one minute, add diced garlic, continue heating for one more minute.

Add garlic, noodles and all ingredients to a large bowl.

Mix well adding Alepo, Ubra Biber, additional oil and vinegar as needed. Noodles should be moist, not wet.

Taste for sufficient level of salt, pepper and herbs. Adjust as needed.

Serve at room temperature as a main course or accompaniment to protein, like quick fried shrimp.

QUICK FRIED SHRIMP (BONUS RECIPE)

1 lb	medium sized wild shrimp, kept in their shells with vein carefully removed
¼	cup vegetable oil
	Salt and fresh ground pepper
½	teaspoon red pepper flakes

Heat oil, add shrimp, fry until crispy, about 3-4 minutes. Mix with salt, ground pepper and red pepper flakes. Delicious added to noodle salad.

THE BERKSHIRE GANG

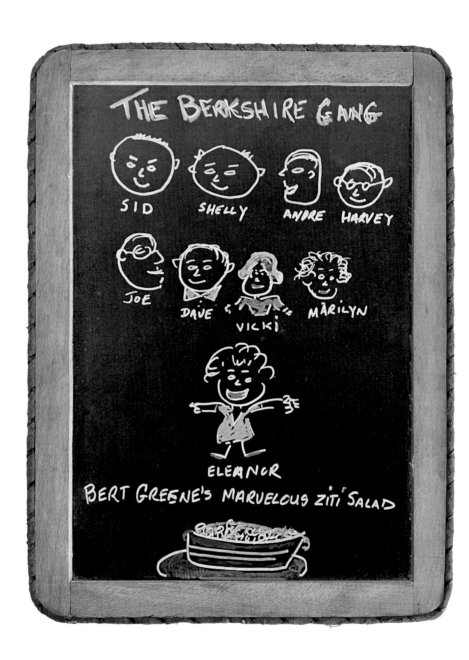

9 SPECIAL PEOPLE

I COULD WRITE page after page about each of these nine special people, so interconnected. Their friendships are bound by creativity and chemistry.

Sid & Shelly, two highly accomplished fine artists. Sid's latest interest in ceramics takes one's breath away. Shelly's paintings invite the viewer to enter the canvas.

Andre & Harvey have reinvented objet d'art, selling one-of-a-kind pieces that could comfortably interface with the zany work of a Jeff Koons or Damien Hirst.

Eleanor is an award-winning designer, writer, a wonderful storyteller. The writing world agrees, more and more of her pieces winning praise and recognition.

Joe & Dave—we call them the farm boys—and farmers they've become. Farming is a respite from Dave's active career as a songwriter, singer, playwright and producer, and Joe a successful software engineer who, in his spare time, makes the most delicious plum jam you've ever tasted.

And finally, Vicki & Marilyn. Vicki is a street photographer whose work can best be compared to Vivian Maier or Dorothea Lange. Marilyn is a PhD, DC, RN, FAAN.

This is our Berkshire Gang. For a pot luck at Eleanor's, I made a dish near and dear to my heart, my spin on Bert Greene's Ziti Salad.

A SPIN ON BERT GREENE'S ZITI SALAD

Along with his influential Wednesday food section for the *New York Daily News*, Bert Greene opened a take-out place in Amagansett called The Store. It was the late 70's. I shed a tear when I remember Bert, clothed in a white shirt and apron that matched the crisp white walls of The Store. Its glass display cabinets housed salads, ham, chicken, roast beef, cakes, and pies.

Stopping on the way to the beach, folks came with lunch baskets. It was a time when Amagansett and East Hampton still had its local rural character.

A picnic from Bert's always included his Ziti Salad, slices of his wonderful baked ham and a crispy baguette.

INGREDIENTS

1½	lb ziti
1	large cucumber, cut in round ¼-inch slices, then halved
2	medium half-sour pickles, cut in round ¼-inch slices then halved
4	fat scallions, diced including green stems
1	large red bell pepper, thinly sliced
½	cup red wine vinegar
½	cup mayo
⅓	cup olive oil
2	tablespoons Herbs de Provence or herbs of your choice, like basil or thyme
1	teaspoon dried oregano
	Salt and ground pepper to taste
½	bunch flat-leaf parsley, chopped

PREP

Boil large pot of water, add tablespoon of salt. Cook ziti following package directions.

Drain ziti, transfer immediately to large bowl. Add olive oil, mix well. Add the balance of ingredients, mix well.

Serve at room temperature, with a selection of protein, e.g. baked ham, cold roast chicken, roast beef, baked salmon, or grilled shrimp.

It's a party! I can smell the Atlantic when I imagine Bert contributing the fare on a gorgeous summer day.

A SIGN IN THE WINDOW

AMONG MY various talents, waiting tables was never a strong suit. So, during the summer of '59, after a short stint as a waiter in the Catskill's Borscht Belt, I was demoted to busboy, having spilled a tray of spaghetti and meatballs all over the hotel's owner, Mr. Shrulowitz, who on a Friday night was wearing a white dinner jacket.

On the spot I went from waiter to busboy, then assigned to Justin, a seasoned summertime Catskill waiter who just finished his last year of podiatry school and was on his last stint in the Borscht Belt.

Justin became my mentor, not only in dining room etiquette but at the time when I needed advice from a big brother. He went on to become an acclaimed foot doctor as well as pioneering entrepreneur in the newly emerging market for orthodic devices.

As time passed we traveled in different directions and lost touch. Then one day, about 20 years later, while walking on Park Avenue I passed a well-known shoe store displaying a sign in the window:

"Here today, Dr. Justin Wernick, noted podiatrist.

Join a clinic on feet and fit."

The store was packed with observers. I took a seat in the back. There was Justin, speaking from the podium. Our eyes met. Now, my dear friend is in my life again. Thank goodness for signage. I continue to learn from him.

And, here's something he can learn from me, an amazing touch to salads and more.

SHALLOT GARLIC DRESSING
(Enough to use with multiple meals)

The shallots both absorb and infuse the other ingredients, making this dressing the perfect accompaniment to a mix of gem lettuce, romaine and arugula. One of my favorite dressings, it can double as an accompaniment sauce over sauteed vegetables, splashed over a simple combination of haricot verts, a woodsy mix of chanterelles, shiitake and cremini mushrooms, satisfying to the most devoted carnivore.

INGREDIENTS

6   oz. good virgin olive oil

1   large shallot, sliced horizontally

3   large garlic cloves minced then finely diced

2   tablespoons red wine vinegar

   Juice from 1/2 lemon (don't forget to remove seeds)

1   tablespoon Dijon mustard

4   good grinds of black pepper

1   teaspoon sea salt

PREP

Transfer all ingredients to a Mason jar with lid. Shake vigorously. Adjust ingredients to your taste.

Add to a choice of greens or veggies, a tablespoon at a time, mix well.

SAMBO STARTED IT ALL

SAM MOCKBEE, Sambo as he was called, dedicated his life to creating architecture that not only elevated the living standards of the rural poor, but, as he would say, "provided shelter for the soul."

My daughter, Mindy, interviewed Sambo for a white paper she was writing on sustainable architecture. That interview evolved into a deep friendship with him and his family that went on well after her report was published.

Sambo had contracted leukemia earlier in his life. Ultimately, he lost the fight against it. Mindy was asked to speak at his memorial.

Stephen, who graduated from Auburn University in Alabama where Mockbee taught, was a member of Sambo's acclaimed work-study program, The Rural Studio. Stephen was also a friend of Sambo and his family.

Stephen in the audience at Sambo's memorial, had an epiphany when he heard Mindy's name, when she was introduced to speak. He thought, *"Oh, that's Mindy Fox!"*

Shortly thereafter Mindy called to tell me she met a *"smart"* carpenter. A year later they married.

Now 18 years later, Mindy and Stephen live in Portland, Maine, with Jasper, my beloved Grand Dog.

Stephen is an award-winning architect, Mindy a successful food writer and publicist. While Mindy knows her way around a kitchen and Stephen never goes hungry, I can always wow them with my Beer Can Chicken.

Wish Sambo was at the table—he started it all.

BEER CAN CHICKEN

This is a guaranteed method for a crispy, moist, delicious chicken with a minimum of preparation. You can use a beer can half filled, or invest in a wonderful substitute: Weber's Poultry Roaster, about $45 and worth every penny.

INGREDIENTS

3-4 lbs organic chicken, gizzards and liver removed. Ask butcher to secure legs and wings around body of the bird.

Fill the cup of the poultry roaster with beer or wine if you decide to purchase the poultry roasting device, otherwise use a half-filled beer can.

2 garlic cloves, sliced

2 tablespoons vegetable cooking oil

Create a dry rub using:

1 teaspoon paprika

1 teaspoon cumin

1 tablespoon dry sage, thyme or rosemary or a bit of each

1 tablespoon kosher salt

4 good grinds of black pepper

Pre-heat grill to 400°, if using a gas grill with 3 burners, leave center burner off.

While grill is heating, prepare the bird for roasting.

Wash chicken outside and inside cavity with cold water, then thoroughly pat down with paper towels.

Insert slices of garlic under skin of bird, careful not to tear skin. Pat kosher salt, grinds of pepper and dry rub thoroughly over skin, then sprinkle with vegetable oil.

You're now ready to place the bird *at attention*, by inserting ½ filled beer can in its cavity so that the bottom of the can acts as a platform. The bird now stands upright. Place standing bird on top of a small pan to catch drippings. (If you've purchased the Weber roaster, no beer can or pan is needed; it has its own.)

Pre-heat grill to 400° degrees.

Transfer bird to grill. Close grill cover. Maintain temperature during grilling at 400° degrees. Set timer at 35 minutes.

Test doneness using temperature gauge inserted at thickest part of body. Temp should read 165° when ready.

Remove bird from grill. Let stand for 10 minutes before transferring to cutting board.

Spoon drippings over bird (the au jus). Delight in the taste of a moist and delicious chicken. Accompany with roasted potatoes and green vegetables.

THE MAESTRO & THE VIDEO ARTIST

BEING INVITED for a meal at David's and Terri's beautiful Scandinavian hilltop house is always a pleasure.

Our last visit was highlighted by a warm borscht David served with a dollop of sour cream offered w/wo horseradish. *Magnifique!*

Along with dinner we discussed their latest concert tour, this time in Portugal. David's musical compositions paired with Terri's video art. The Portuguese were wowed as were we, reminded of the special collaborations these two wonderful people create.

David is an octogenarian hipster, a cutting-edge artist, an Art Garfunkel look-alike, only cuter.

David, I call him Maestro, for that is who he is, a composer and pioneer of digital music. He has had long associations with John Cage, Merce Cunningham, and Jasper Johns, among others.

Terri is a video artist whose work integrates music, lighting, costumes, places, and people.

David grew up in an artistic world. His father was S. N. Behrman, a well-known screenwriter, Broadway playwright and *New Yorker* contributor. His mother, Elza Heifetz, was a sister of violinist Jascha Heifetz. His nephew, Peter Gelb, is the much talked about General Manager of the Metropolitan Opera.

I could listen to David for hours talking about Leonard Bernstein, Arturo Toscanini, Jascha Heifetz, Cary Grant, to name a few, who met at his boyhood home.

David thinks I make the best meatballs he's ever tasted. The secret's in the sauce.

MEATBALLS IN TOMATO SAUCE WITH BLACK INK PASTA

Cooking pasta reminds me of my generous, loving dad, a guy who could eat pasta every day. I was often left to make dinner for him and Mom. After she returned from her day job, and Dad awoke to eat before leaving for the night shift, we met at the dinner table. Spaghetti and meatballs became my specialty.

INGREDIENTS (Meatballs)

1 ½	lbs mix of ground beef, veal and pork
¼	cup each: chopped fresh basil, rosemary and parsley
1	tablespoon dry oregano
1	teaspoon each cinnamon and allspice
6	cloves fresh garlic, diced
2	tablespoons unflavored bread crumbs or panko
1	teaspoon ground pepper
1	tablespoon kosher salt
2	eggs slightly beaten
½	cup olive oil
½	medium onion, chopped

PREP (Meatballs)

In a food processor combine all the fresh herbs with the onion and garlic. Add a tablespoon olive oil, blend for 10 seconds (give or take). You want the ingredients to be well combined.

Now combine chopped meat and all ingredients in a medium mixing bowl. Mix well.

With a large tablespoon, portion out about 8 meatballs, carefully hand roll.

Heat half the oil in a large pan. Add meatballs and sauté over medium heat, turning until golden brown, about ten minutes. Set meatballs aside while preparing sauce.

SAUCE →

INGREDIENTS (Sauce)

1	28 oz. can San Marzano tomatoes
3	tablespoons dry oregano
1	teaspoon each of cinnamon, allspice and Aleppo pepper
5	cloves garlic, finely chopped
½	cup olive oil
	Salt and fresh ground pepper
1	large onion, chopped
1	red and
1	yellow bell pepper, seeds removed and thinly sliced
1	cup water. Use small amounts as needed
1	lb fresh or dry squid ink pasta
1	cup shaved Parmigiano cheese

PREP (Sauce)

In a large sauté pan, heat half the olive oil. Add the onion, red and yellow peppers.

Continue cooking on low-medium flame until onions are opaque and peppers soften. Add chopped garlic, cook gently for 3 minutes.

Add can of tomatoes, herbs and spices, turn heat up a notch, continue cooking until ingredients begin to simmer.

With a wooden spoon, chop tomatoes as they cook.

Add meatballs.

Cook for 40 minutes, adding small amounts of water if sauce gets too thick.

While meatballs are cooking, boil pasta following package instructions, short of 3 minutes.

Add pasta to cooked meatballs and sauce, continue cooking for an additional 3-4 minutes. Mix well.

Plate pasta and meatballs with plenty of sauce. Sprinkle with chopped parsley and shaved Parmigiano.

HERB

HE'S A STORYTELLER

I MET HERB at Mt. Sinai Hospital's maternity floor awaiting the delivery of Mindy, my first born. Herb was awaiting the arrival of his first child, Marc. There was plenty of time for two expectant fathers to talk. As I would soon learn, Herb was an insurance man. He immediately scoped me out as a prospect. He sold me a $10,000 life insurance policy, there and then. "Now you're a family man."

Our meeting, and my buying an insurance policy, didn't end there. Herb and I bought our first homes blocks from one another in New Jersey. His second child, Greg, and mine, Jason, arrived at about the same time.

Over the years we never tired of telling stories about our time in the Army Reserve, awaiting deployment. When I moved to New Hampshire, I left behind with Herb a BMW to sell. It wasn't a snow car.

Oh, the times we enjoyed cooking together. Herbie's famous "Thanksgiving at Christmas" dinners:

4-5 hors d' oeuvres, 2 soups, baked ham, turkey, roast beef, both sweet potatoes mashed and baked potatoes, at least 3 kinds of cranberry sauce, 3 or 4 vegetable dishes, 2 salads, 3 kinds of pie

Now, in our 80s, no longer working in jobs we loved, deciding it's time to stop skiing, to downsize, to sell houses we were living in for decades.

Moving: never easy. Dislodging boxes of ancient photos and memorabilia. Memories of joys, accomplishments, disappointments, losses, discoveries. The fodder for a contemporary version of *Gone with the Wind*. This one about two Jewish boys, one growing up in Queens, the other in the Bronx. Herb's dad selling kosher chickens. My dad, a truck driver, delivering meat.

Life is life. There's nothing better than elevating the spirits by sharing a delicious slice of matzo brei with a dollop of sour cream.

MATZO BREI WITH SOUR CREAM

My Polish mom's life lesson: *"When you're expecting company, fry some chopped onions about a half hour before they arrive. Boom! The smell of the onions makes your guests immediately feel welcomed."*

Mom was a master of Judeo-Eastern European wisdom. What I took from her, among many other things, was a love for fried onions.

As you see, they're in my Matzo Brei.

INGREDIENTS

1	tablespoon cube of butter
¼	cup olive oil
1	large onion, chopped
6	pieces of matzo, broken into two-inch pieces
½	cup milk
2	eggs, well beaten
1	teaspoon ground pepper
½	teaspoon salt

PREP

Heat half the butter and oil in a large frying pan. Add onion, cook until translucent going on brown. Careful not to burn.

Add matzo, milk, eggs, onions, and seasoning to a large mixing bowl. Mix well.

Add a bit more butter and oil to the pan. Turn up heat to medium-high.

When pan is well heated, pour out contents of mixing bowl into the pan and spread it out.

Slightly reduce flame, continue cooking about 5 minutes, then check to see if matzo begin to crisp. When it does, you can flip the matzo. If it breaks up, don't worry. You just want all sides of the matzo brei to be browned and crispy.

Cook for an additional 3-4 minutes. Serve with a dollop of sour cream. Add chopped scallions to the sour cream for more flavor.

THE CHEF & THE CHEESE MONGER

I MET THESE extraordinary women through my daughter, all of them denizens of the food world.

Mona Talbott earned her chops working with Alice Waters at Chez Panisse in Berkeley, before going on to take over as Executive Chef of the American Academy in Rome and its Sustainable Food Project.

Kate Arding, a native of England, began her career as a cheese monger at *Neal's Yard*, a dairy in London, before relocating to California, where she helped establish *Cowgirl Creamery*. As described by her peers, Kate is among the world's leading cheese experts.

Mona and Kate met, discovering they had a shared vision to create, produce, distribute, and sell the finest food available anywhere.

They sought outside branding advice, and that's where I came in. It was the easiest assignment I'd ever tackled. To me, their surnames, Talbot and Arding, said it all.

After a lot of thought, and, I'm sure, getting multiple opinions, Mona and Kate agreed. It would be,

Talbott & Arding, Cheese and Provisions

What better name for the *best-of-the-best* food purveyor founded by an extraordinary chef and the world's leading cheese monger. Now into their seventh year and a new 8,000+ sq. ft. space, their names do their business proud.

They arrived for dinner, "Flanken? What's that?"

FLANKEN

This recipe, contributed by Ellen Rudley, is one that my Yiddish Momma made. Ellen's flanken is even better than I remember Mom's to be. Think of flanken (beef short ribs) as Jewish beef stew.

INGREDIENTS

8	pieces of flanken
2-3	marrow bones
2	stalks celery
2	carrots
1	large onion
1	clove, stuck in onion
1	bay leaf
½	pound fresh mushrooms
½	cup dried mixed mushrooms
8	cups water
1	cup barley
	Salt and pepper
	White horseradish, as a condiment

PREP

Rinse flaken, remove excess fat.

Put flanken and marrow bones in a pot of water, covering meat 2-3 inches. Boil, skimming fat. Continuing cooking on simmer. Add carrots, onion, celery and bay leaf.

Simmer for about 2 hours until meat is fork-tender. Cool. Refrigerate overnight.

Remove from fridge and skim fat from surface. Remove celery, carrots, onion and bay leaf. Add mushrooms. Reheat to light boil for another 20 minutes.

While meat is reheating, boil barley separately following package instructions.

When barley is done, add to meat and veggies.

Now you're ready to serve it. Use soup bowls. Accompany with a condiment of white horseradish.

CHARLES & BETH

LUNCH AT THE WANA-WANA CLUB

I WILL FOREVER hold dear visits at their three-story, 19th century clapboard house overlooking Little Narraganset Bay, off Stonington Borough. A wonderful, inviting house bordered by Beth's extraordinary gardens, the perfect spot for morning coffee. *Magnifique!*

On afternoons we'd climb to the third-floor of the house, up a steep staircase opening to the generous studio space they created. The wide windows faced a small harbor whose view changed with time and tide.

Downstairs, I remember the living room, walls painted in salmon, anointed with Beth's wonderful still life and landscapes, sharing space with the other carefully selected paintings.

The over-stuffed sofa and chairs called out for a cocktail before meal time then again for a post-dinner single malt, bookending Beth's delicious dinner. The night's conversation crossed a wide multitude of subjects, including our time in advertising.

Lunch. Occasionally at Noah's, a local cafe on Water Street, or more often, the Wadawanuck Club, where Charles moored his Boston Whaler and sailboat, people played tennis, kids swam off the small beach, ladies lunched (sometimes with their husbands).

Like most things in Stonington, the Wadawanuck Club is a tradition. I rebranded it the Wana-Wana.

Fare at the Wana-Wana was simple. Hot dogs, tuna on white, chicken or egg salad, every choice accompanied by a pickle and handful of *Pringles* potato chips, served by acne-crusted high schoolers on summer break.

Dear memories, dearest friends, many more mealtimes together.

Dinner for the Hardings includes pork chops. (Charles's meal must include a meat dish.) Complementing the chop, a baked August peach.

GRILLED PORK CHOPS

Forget the old wife's tale, pork must be cooked well done, unless you want something hard to chew and swallow. Here's the way to make a pork chop juicy and succulent.

INGREDIENTS

4   bone-in pork chops, one for each guest

3   garlic cloves, smashed with the blade of a knife

1   tablespoon fresh rosemary, chopped

1   tablespoon fresh sage, chopped

1   tablespoon olive oil

PREP

Add garlic, rosemary, sage and olive oil to food processor. Pulse for 30 seconds. Spread marinade over both sides of chops. Refrigerate for 1 hour or overnight.

Pre-heat grill pan to 500°. Add chops. Grill for 3½ minutes, then flip, and grill for an additional 3½ minutes. Total 7 minutes (no more).

Remove chops from the heat, let rest for ten minutes. Serve with grilled peaches for a surprising alternative to veggies.

BAKED AUGUST PEACHES →

BAKED AUGUST PEACHES

"Simple" best describes this delicious accompaniment to a main course in summer.

INGREDIENTS

4	medium ripe yellow peaches, sliced in half, pits removed
1	tablespoon cinnamon, enough to lightly sprinkle 8 peach haves
1	teaspoon Aleppo pepper
¼	cup olive oil
1	tablespoon honey
¼	cup chopped mint

PREP

Place peach halves on lightly oiled pan.

Heat oven or grill to 400° degrees.

Drip a little olive oil and a few drops of honey on each peach half.

Sprinkle peach halves with cinnamon and Aleppo.

Place peaches in oven face up. Bake for 10 minutes or until edges crisp.

WHAT EAVESDROPPING GOT ME

I MET JOHN and Pam in Chicago in 1975, seated at a nearby table in a very nice restaurant. It was late in the lunch service, and only a few stragglers remained. I enjoyed hearing their British accents, and perked up when they mentioned people and places that were familiar to me.

By lunch's end I grew more intrigued and got up the nerve to ask if we shared aquaintances. Turned out that we did. John and I were both ad guys. A friendship began that has continued to this day, despite the geography (US to Spain) between us.

John and Pam steered me to destinations I'd probably never go—wonderful places where they've lived. Tepoztlán, south of Mexico City. Santiago, Chile. Paraty in Brazil. Blackheath, a small village outside of London. And, more recently, their home in Solarius, in Spain's Sierra Nevada.

They kept horses, dogs and cats. I remember John and me galloping across a high mountain plateau in Chile, feeling a deep companionship.

Whenever and wherever we are together, it's time to cook. While Pam has few equals in the kitchen, she loves my Camarones con Salsa Verde.

All this because I eavesdropped at a restaurant in Chicago.

CAMARONES CON SALSA VERDE

One of my favorite, easy-to-prepare dishes. And, to get raves from Pam, one of the best chefs I know, is an endorsement par excellence.

INGREDIENTS

1 ½	lbs wild caught shrimp
½	cup olive oil
1	cup cilantro
1	cup parsley
4	cloves garlic chopped
1	teaspoon Aleppo pepper
1	teaspoon kosher salt
4	good grinds of black pepper
1	large onion, chopped
1	red bell pepper cut in thin strips
1 ½	cups basmati rice

PREP

Start by cooking rice.

Rinse rice. Boil 3 cups of water. Add rice. Cook covered for 20 minutes.

While rice is cooking, remove vein from shrimp and butterfly, keeping shell on. See page 89 for instructions.

In a food processor add garlic, half the olive oil, cilantro, parsley, Aleppo pepper, salt and black pepper. Pulse for 30 seconds.

In a large frying pan, on medium flame, heat balance of olive oil, add onion and red pepper. Sauté until onion becomes transparent and red pepper begins to blister, about 5 minutes.

Add butterflyed shrimp to pan, sauté until they turn pink, 3-4 minutes.

Add contents of food processor, lower flame, continue to cook for 2 minutes. Mix well.

Your Camarones con Salsa Verde is ready.

Plate individual portions over rice.

Delicioso!

ALICE KEPT HIM ON POINT

FOR MORE THAN 50 years, Erard and I spoke almost every day. A Brit, he came to the US in the early 60's after graduating from Oxford. We met soon after, both of us landing our first jobs, working in the bullpen of a big, stodgy ad agency.

Erard soon left advertising, enrolled at Columbia Law School, got his law degree, then landed a job working for Robert Kennedy at the Bed Stuy Restoration Project. When Kennedy was assassinated, Erard was out of a job.

I suggested he join the ad agency I was now working for. Erard came aboard. We did great work and had great fun doing it.

Simpatico is the word that best describes our relationship. For half a century and four company iterations we continued working together until the unbelievable occurred, Erard contracted Alzheimer's.

Erard was always the brilliant, absent-minded professor and Alice, his wonderful, loving, brainy wife was always there to keep him on point. Now she was there for him day and night.

My last memory of Erard was of him and me walking along a Connecticut beach, now in his fifth year with Alzheimer's. We conversed, in a manner, me doing all the talking. He didn't know my name, but I was sure he knew me in some way.

I asked him, "Erard, remember that bastard Neil Fox?"

"Oh," he said. "He wasn't such a bad guy."

Erard, being a Brit, loved Indian food. For him, Chicken Curry.

CHICKEN CURRY

Erard always ordered a beer and a coke. He never ate much, but he did like curry. I guess a throwback from England's colonization of India. That said, Erard was far from a colonizer. The illustration on the chalkboard is of me, not Erard. He'd never don a mustache or a bow tie.

INGREDIENTS

1 ½	pound boneless chicken thighs, cut into ¾ inch cubes
½	cup olive oil
2	large onions, chopped
1	teaspoon salt
4	good grinds of pepper
2	tablespoons curry powder
1	tablespoon garam masala
1	13 oz can unsweetened coconut milk
1	cup diced tomatoes
½	cup chopped cilantro
2	cups basmati rice

PREP

Add oil to large sauté pan, heat on medium flame, add onions, salt and pepper. Cook until onions turn translucent, about 5 minutes.

Add curry and garam masala, mix for another minute.

Add chicken, cook for another 8 minutes at low to medium flame. Add coconut milk, continue cooking, 3-4 minutes.

Add tomato, cook for another 2 minutes.

Cut piece of chicken to check doneness. Taste to adjust seasonings as necessary.

Serve over basmati rice* and mango chutney. Garnish with cilantro.

* See page 69 for directions on cooking rice.

TERRY & DOUGLAS

WE CLICKED

IT'S A RARE occurrence when you meet another couple at a cocktail party and know instantly the chemistry is right. So it was for Ellen and me the day we met Douglas and Terry.

Instead of talking about health and grandchildren, topics that immediately trigger a desire in me to escape, we discussed real issues.

Douglas and I exchanged views on the Middle East. He is chairman of an organization that seeks to build a dialogue for peace among Palestinian and Israeli families. (*Wow, how does that work?*)

I heard about the time he met Benny Goodman, who encouraged his learning to play the clarinet. I also heard about his year abroad after graduating college, marked by a fling with an Air France hostess. While in Israel, he was invited to a party and met Moshe Dayan. On and on.

Ellen and Terry realized their fathers had worked for the same company, in similar jobs at similar times and probably knew each other. She and Ellen were actively working with nonprofits and were vegetarians. Now marked by years of laughter, we've forged a deep friendship.

Shortly after Covid hit and it was safe to travel, we decided to take a short vacation together. We picked St. Petersburg, FL. The day we arrived at our pink, 1920's stucco monolith of a hotel (I dubbed it the Don Corleone), we headed to the resort's beach. There we were set up on chaises next to a rather generous-sized Southern woman. She engaged us in conversation, a restaurant she recommended, "It's got a whole room just devoted to desserts." We exchanged a glance. Then came questions. "Where are you all from?" Douglas answered, "New York". "Oh, are you Democrats? Do you believe in the bible, God?" Before she could don her MAGA cap we took off for a walk. When we returned, she was gone.

Such was the start of our three days in St. Pete's. As soon as we got home, Douglas and Terry came over for dinner. Ravioli with sage butter. But, no dessert.

RAVIOLI AND SAGE BUTTER

Just minutes to prepare. And, most important, it's a vegetarian's delight. Another thing Terry and Ellen have in common.

INGREDIENTS

28	medium sized raviolis (filling of your choice).
½	stick of butter
¼	cup olive oil
1	bunch fresh sage, leaves chopped, stems removed.
	Large pot of water
2	tablespoons Kosher salt
	Juice from half lemon
1	teaspoon sea salt, more for final tasting
½	cup shredded Parmigiano Reggiano
¼	teaspoon cinnamon (optional)

Note: I get my ravioli fresh from Eately or Borgatti's, a 100 year-old pasta store located in the Arthur Avenue section of the Bronx

PREP

Fill a large pot 3/4 full of water, add 2 tablespoons kosher salt. Boil. Then add ravioli.

Cook ravioli on boil, about 14 minutes. Taste for doneness. Ravioli should be medium soft, easily digestible.

While ravioli is cooking, add together butter and olive oil. Warm mixture in small pot, until butter melts. Keep mixture warm. Careful not to burn.

When ravioli is ready, drain in colander, transfer to large sized serving bowl. Immediately pour butter/oil mixture over ravioli. Mix well.

Mix in chopped sage, several grinds of peppercorns, a few sprinkles of sea salt and lemon juice.

Sprinkle with lemon juice.

The final step, add shaved cheese.

Serve family style with a simple green salad.

Mangiare!

JOEL & JUDIE

LOVE THY NEIGHBOR

A PATH THROUGH the woods has connected our houses. We kept the path mowed, clear of fallen trees and branches. It marks the connection between us.

We've been neighbors going on 12 years. Almost every day, one of us has crossed the path to the other's house.

It started when we found our house, a hidden gem built in the 50's in need of a lot of loving care. It took nine months to bring it back to its original beautiful self. All along, Joel and Judie were observing, listening graciously to the noisy construction crew, wondering who would be their neighbors. The day we moved in Judie knocked on the door with a plate of cookies.

Since then, Joel and I have tried to walk most days when weather allows, usually three miles. We begin at my house, get to the end of the driveway, then make a big decision, do we go right or left?

Judie is a warm, charming, caring individual. She's taught us to play RummyQ and dominoes. I know Canasta is next. On these long Covid winters, what better way to enjoy our friendship.

In addition to sharing a proverbial cup of sugar we've relied on Joel for his technical and medical expertise—he is a retired doc. He can set up a new computer and fix a printer. I reciprocate by cooking eggplant Parm for Joel or a creative salad from Mindy Fox's *Salads: Beyond the Bowl* cookbook, like "Watercress, avocado, and grapefruit salad with tarragon-shallot vinegar."

Alas, as I pen this chapter, Joel and Judie have decided to down-size. Luckily the condo they bought is only 20 minutes away, not the same as just crossing a path, but we will have new trails to walk and conquer. And, who knows, the new neighbors may provide the ingredients for another chalkboard.

WATERCRESS, AVOCADO, AND GRAPEFRUIT SALAD WITH TARRAGON-SHALLOT VINEGAR

I continue to be astonished by Mindy, my daughter, her knowledge, creativity, and writing acumen. She has authored, co-authored and contributed to upwards of twenty cookbooks, including projects with Gail Simmons, food expert and judge on the Emmy-winning series, *Top Chef*, and Antoni Porowski, Emmy award-winning food and wine expert on the Netflix smash hit, *Queer Eye*. Mindy wrote 'the book' on salads called, *Salads: Beyond the Bowl*. Here's one of my favorite recipes. Judie loves it!

INGREDIENTS

(For the vinaigrette)

- 1 tablespoon chopped shallot
- 1 tablespoon champagne vinegar
  Fine sea salt
- 1 teaspoon white pepper corns, crushed
- 3 tablespoons very good olive oil
- 2 tablespoons finely chopped tarragon, plus 2 tablespoons whole leaves for garnish

(For the salad)

- 1 large grapefruit or 2 small ones
- 1 firm-ripe avocado
- 1 large bunch watercress
- 2 pinches flaky coarse sea salt

PREP

Crush the whole white pepper corns by pressing the bottom of a heavy skillet against them. This makes a coarser flake and robust burst of flavor than using a pepper grinder.

In a medium bowl, stir together the shallot, vinegar, $1/4$ teaspoon fine sea salt, crushed white pepper corns, and let stand for 10 minutes.

Using a paring knife, peel grapefruit and cut into sections. Squeeze the juice out of the membranes and discard.

Cut the avocado into quarters lengthwise, remove the pit and peel. Cut into $1/4$ inch thick slices. Drizzle with the grapefruit juice and season with a pinch of sea salt and white pepper.

Divide the watercress among 4 serving plates. Arrange the avocado and grapefruit slices on top.

Add oil and chopped tarragon to the shallot mixture and vigorously whisk to combine, then spoon the dressing over the salad. Sprinkle with tarragon leaves and pinches of salt and pepper, then crush a generous pinch or two of flaky course sea salt over the top.

MY MEAT LOAF ONLY SCORED A 4!

I'VE KNOWN Judy and Thad for as long as I've known Ellen. I didn't get to know the 'real' Judy until she and Thad decided to leave Martha's Vineyard (MV), where they lived for 20 years, and move to our neck of the woods.

There began the saga.

Judy and Thad are my vintage. They bought a new home in the Berkshires, renovated it, then decided, soon after moving in they didn't like where it was located. They sold the house.

While this was going on, in addition to her psychotherapy practice, Judy opened her MV clothing store Red Mannequin in nearby Hudson, New York, then decided she didn't like that location either.

Within weeks, they found and bought a new house in their favorite town, Chatham. The new house needed a new kitchen, bath, front porch and landscaping, and while this was going on Judy looked and found a new store. It needed a makeover as well.

Thad, amazing man that he is, keeps up with Judy's endless energy. In addition to being a skilled handyman, he's an accomplished psychologist with clients that follow him wherever Judy decides to settle. And, he's just completed a book on the subject of insomnia.

Judy and (especially) Thad deserve a good night's sleep. Something Thad's new book *The Fight for Sleep** will insure.

Judy liked my meatloaf but, she only scored it a 4 out of 5. I need to try harder.

Hoping this new recipe for turkey meatloaf will earn a '5'.

---

* *The Fight for Sleep* is available at amazon.com.

TURKEY MEAT LOAF (HOPING FOR A 5)

Working hard for a 5 from Judy.
I thought I made a mean meat loaf until Judy ranked it 4 out of 5.

I definitely needed to improve. After searching cooks and cookbooks I came up with a totally new approach.

INGREDIENTS

2	tablespoons olive oil
1/4	cup Pinot Grigio, or any other white is fine
1	cup diced onions
1	tablespoon minced garlic
1/4	cup bread crumbs
1 1/2	lbs ground turkey
1	egg, lightly beaten
3	minced, then diced garlic cloves
1	teaspoon kosher salt
3	grinds black pepper
1	teaspoon paprika
1/2	teaspoon allspice
1	teaspoon dried thyme
1	tablespoon fresh chopped sage
1	teaspoon dried oregano
1	cup fresh parsley, chopped
3/4	cup ketchup

PREP

Pre-heat oven to 400°.

In a skillet, heat olive oil, add onions, cook until onions are browned.

Add fried onions, turkey and all ingredients (reserving half the parsley and half the ketchup) to a large bowl. Mix throughly.

Shape the meat mixture into a loaf. Place loaf in a high rimmed ceramic or steel pan sized to give the loaf a small bit of room.

Reduce oven heat to 350°. Cook for 35 minutes or until a meat thermometer reaches 155°.

Thinly spread the remaining ketchup on top of the loaf, bake for an additional 10 minutes.

Remove pan from oven and allow it to rest for 20 minutes.

Sprinkle loaf with remaining parsley.

Perfect, accompanied by a baked potato and chopped spinach.

Voila! Fingers crossed while awaiting Judy's approval.

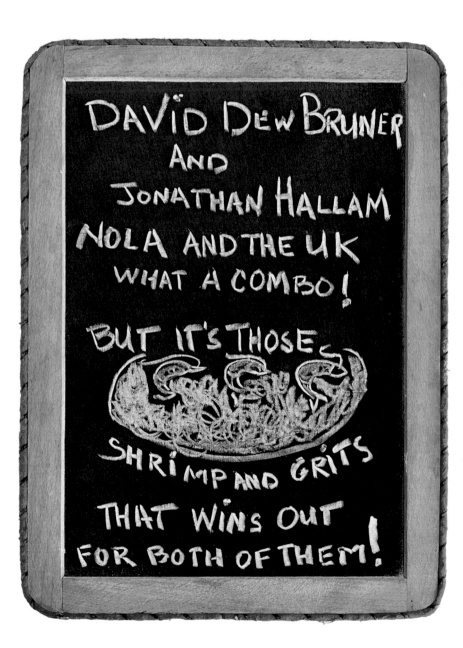

CONTRAPUNTO

CONTRAPUNTO OR COUNTERPOINT is a phrase in music that describes two harmonically interdependent, yet independent melodic contours, each melody complimenting the other.

That's how it is with David and Hallam.

David's voice sings of his hometown, New Orleans. Hallam, a Brit, speaks "proper" English. (No Cockney accent in evidence here) Together their voices enrich the lives of all who know them.

David is an extraordinarily gifted artist. A painting of his, the reimaging of Velázquez's *Infanta*, hangs on my living room wall, in a black rococo frame. I could lose myself for hours in its vision of 17th century Spain.

David's artwork is equal to his genius as a landscape designer, all of which comes through in his booming Louisiana accent.

Hallam has a special eye for design evident in his fire engine red Alfa Romeo, Julia. In addition to his ability to find exquisite examples of 19th and 20th century furniture and related art pieces, he has occupied several amazing houses since I've known him, including a rare Octagon House, the historic Rensselaer mansion. The Federal-style Turtle House is where he has a showroom, welcoming a list of avid clients to view and purchase objects, whose provenance he delivers with an authoritative English accent.

Given David's affinity for cooking, among his other talents, I'm preparing a dish famous in his home town, New Orleans, Shrimp and Grits.

SHRIMP AND GRITS

One of the easiest to prepare, most delicious dishes on my list. Shrimp and grits: hard to beat. Enjoy it with beer, a hearty red, or dry Riesling.

INGREDIENTS

1	cup polenta (corn meal)
3	cups water
1 ½	pounds, shell-on Louisiana wild caught shrimp
1	thinly sliced red or yellow bell pepper, seeds removed
½	medium onion, sliced
¼	cup olive oil
3	cloves garlic, chopped
1	tablespoon sriracha
1	tablespoon chives
1	tablespoon parsley
	Salt and pepper

PREP

Boil 3 cups water. While water is boiling, devein shrimp. Leaving the shell on, butterfly shrimp by pressing the sliced area open against the cutting board.

When water reaches a boil, slowly add polenta. Cook for about 7 minutes, mixing to reduce clumping. Taste for doneness.

Heat oil in sauté pan sufficient in size to hold shrimp.

Add sliced pepper and onion, sauté on medium flame until pepper begins to blister. Add shrimp and increase flame. Continue cooking until shrimp turn pink.

Add sriracha, lower flame. Cook, stirring for 3 minutes.

Place a scoop of polenta on each plate. Top with shrimp, peppers and onions (approximately 6 shrimp per serving).

Add a grind of black pepper to each serving. Sprinkle with chopped chives and parsley.

Serve with dry Riesling or your favorite beer.

INVENTOR OF THE MOOM

AS BEN likes to say, "Neil? He's my mother's boyfriend." His mother, Ellen, and I have been living together for 19 years. You'd think by now I'd have graduated to a more noble descriptor.

But that's Ben, making sure he'll be the one to decide any new title I would earn.

Ben is a creative force. For his real estate biz he branded himself the Neighborhood Guy. Ben's the inside man, who not only can identify a great property, but also the local go-to restaurant, the hip second-hand clothing shop, the local bakery, and the artful tailor.

Ben is a realtor, comedian, actor, writer, music producer, an entrepreneur, a committed student of healthy body and mind. And, did I say, he's the inventor of the Moom.

The Moom, a broom that plays music that you can dance to while sweeping. Now, there's a concept that only Ben could have thought of. It was the centerpiece of a comedy sketch he wrote, *The Spinellis*, that he and his acting partner, Lucy, performed to the joy of an East Village jam-packed theater.

I watch video clips of plays and films that Ben has performed in. What an accomplished artist he has become. He's got a certain something. Well, he is the inventor of the Moom!

He says my Chicken Primavera is the best he's ever had. Given that he eats weekly at Carbone, that's a good compliment.

CHICKEN PRIMAVERA

Chicken is my go-to protein. Healthy and delicious. My preference is usually dark thigh meat, bone-in or out. And, always organic and coming from a reliable source.

If you can buy local that's great. National brands that humanely raise their birds include Bell & Evans and D'Artagnan.

As regards my Chicken Primavera, take note, muenster is an especially nice option to mozzarella.

INGREDIENTS

4	skinless, boneless chicken thighs
1	medium onion, sliced
1	red bell pepper, thinly sliced
4	tablespoons tomato sauce
2	plum tomatoes, sliced
½	cup olive oil
4	cloves garlic, minced
4	slices muenster cheese
½	cup bread crumbs
2	tablespoons dried oregano
1	egg, vigorously beaten
	Salt and freshly ground pepper

Pre-heat oven to 400°.

Dip each chicken thigh into egg, sprinkle salt, grinds of pepper and bread crumbs.

Heat oil. Lightly sauté thighs over medium flame until browned, about 5 minutes. Set thighs aside.

In a high walled, pre-heated baking dish layer ingredients as follows:

$\frac{1}{2}$ tablespoon olive oil, spread across the bottom of the pan
Slices of one tomato to cover pan
Sprinkle of oregano
two browned chicken thighs
2 tablespoons tomato sauce
2 slices of onion and red pepper
Another sprinkle of oregano
2 slices cheese
Another sprinkle of oregano, salt, and a grind of black pepper
Remaining browned chicken thighs
Sliced tomato
2 tablespoons tomato sauce
Remaining onion and red pepper slices
Remaining $\frac{1}{2}$ tablespoon olive oil

Bake at 400° for 35 minutes. Add remaining cheese slices, continue baking for 5 minutes until chess melts.

Let rest for 10 minutes. Watch Ben consume in 5.

EAST SIDE DARLINGS

DAVID AND BUTCH* picked the East Side to live when they arrived in NY from their hometown of St. Louis in the early 60's. Before long they took on the persona of Manhattan chic. They had a certain something that people were drawn to.

They always kept a dog, and in the early days, Siamese cats. In later years, an adopted greyhound or two—very East Side.

They'd always get a front table—their table—at Elio's, where they would nod to the Walter Cronkites seated close by. They would get a hug and kiss from Elaine herself when they arrived at her celebrity haunt and never got snubbed when calling for a reservation at Rao's.

Soon after arriving in the city, David got into the ad biz. That's where we met, two young guys who loved coming up with big ideas.

We personified the creative and strategic shift advertising was taking in the 60's, doing great work for big name clients like Colgate, M&M/Mars, Lego, Matchbox Cars, Melitta, to name a few. Being part of a leading British ad agency didn't hurt. David became the agency's creative team leader.

While David was kept busy, Butch's creative abilities found their way into designing three-dimensional, one of a kind, personalized, much in demand, event invitations.

I called upon her talents to design a mailing piece for my client *AdWeek*. We branded it *AdMan*. It won a coveted One Show award.

David is gone, having lost his battle with Parkinson's. Butch carries the flame, a forever East Side darling.

---

* By the way, Butch is a girl.

GUACAMOLE AND SHRIMP TORTILLAS WITH BLACK BEAN-PINEAPPLE SALSA

Before Rosa Mexicana went big time, we'd go to their first location, on First Ave. and 59th St., for the best guacamole prepared tableside. Now I make one better.

INGREDIENTS (GUACAMOLE)

1	avocado
½	onion, diced
½	jalapeno, diced
	Juice of 1/2 lime
¾	cup chopped cilantro
1	teaspoon olive oil
1	teaspoon Aleppo pepper
	Several good grinds of black pepper
½	teaspoon sea salt

PREP

In a medium-size bowl, combine ingredients. Mix well, careful to keep avocado chunky. Serve with blue corn taco chips.

SHRIMP TORTILLAS AND SALSA →

INGREDIENTS (SHRIMP TORTILLAS AND SALSA)

1	lb. shrimp
½	pineapple, peeled and core removed, cut into ½" pieces
14	oz. can black beans, thoroughly rinsed
½	bunch cilantro, chopped
	Juice of 1 lime
1	teaspoon Aleppo pepper
½	medium onion, diced
1	teaspoon salt
1	teaspoon ground pepper
1	tablespoon olive oil
8	corn tortillas

PREP

In a medium skillet, heat olive oil. Add shrimp, cook until pink, about 5 minutes. Warm tortillas in the oven or use a frying pan (no oil) to toast the tortillas individually.

In a medium bowl combine pineapple, black beans, cilantro, lime juice, Aleppo pepper, diced onion, salt and black pepper. Mix ingredients well and spoon over warmed tortillas.

Add shrimp. Roll up tortillas with ingredients inside, fold ends closed.

Take a bite. Wow, what a combo!

MY PATHFINDER

"**FROM YOUR CHILDREN** you will be taught." These words by Kahlil Gibran touch my heart and soul deeply.

My children are my greatest teachers. This chapter is about my son, my pathfinder.

We've traveled many paths, physically and spiritually—some close by, others far away. Hunting for mushrooms, taking hikes with Jason's dogs, Emma and Zane, skiing and hiking the Rockies, paddling the Colorado, Green and Connecticut rivers, fishing the Atlantic, gazing across Canyonlands, cooking together, eating our way through Umbria.

One year our paths converged at Whistler-Blackcomb, a magnificent destination in the mountains of British Columbia, the start to our week skiing together.

Snowing hard, we planned our first dinner in. We hit the supermarket, filled shopping bags to the brim, then a five-minute drive back to our condo. We parked, each taking two bags from the trunk.

Jason walked slightly ahead. I stepped gingerly behind. Then, I hit an ice patch. Watching, as if in slow-motion, my legs flew up. I felt the crash and heard a crack. The pain was intense. "Oh Poppa, are you OK?"

I wasn't. A fractured ankle. That was it for skiing, for me.

Jason skied in the mornings, then hurried back to stay with me. We played gin, cooked some great meals, laughed a lot. How great it is to experience love and care, not always being in control, not the teacher, to experience my son. My pathfinder.

Now for a grilled New York strip with mushroom sauce, one of our favorite meals.

GRILLED NEW YORK STRIPS WITH MUSHROOM SAUCE

There's nothing better than a grilled steak marinated in red wine and garlic, accompanied by a sauce of wild mushrooms—whatever's available from the forest floor. If the mushrooms are there, Jason will find them.

INGREDIENTS

2	pasture-raised, 2" thick, NY strip steaks
1	heaping tablespoon kosher salt
¼	cup vegetable oil
6	large garlic cloves
2	tablespoons fresh rosemary
½	cup Chianti
1	teaspoon ground pepper
½	pound wild mushrooms, of your choice
2	tablespoons butter
	Salt and pepper

PREP

In a food processor add 1 tablespoon vegetable oil, garlic cloves, rosemary (stems removed), pepper, and kosher salt. Process for about 15 seconds until ingredients are chunky. Rub steaks with a thick covering of the processed ingredients.

Transfer steaks to a medium sized ceramic pan, just large enough to fit them. Add Chianti.

Marinate in fridge for several hours or overnight, turning steaks from time to time.

Preheat grill to 500°.

Add steaks. With top closed, grill each side 3½ minutes for medium-rare. Spoon marinade over steaks as they are turned.

Transfer to a cutting board to rest 10 minutes.

While steaks are resting, heat butter in a sauté pan. Add mushrooms and several good grinds of pepper.

Sauté mushrooms for 10 minutes on low flame. Top each steak with mushrooms and dig in.

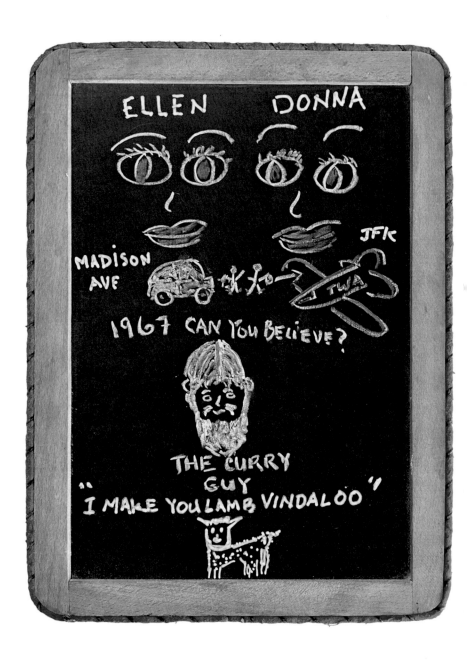

$50. A LOT OF MONEY IN THOSE DAYS

WHEN I LOOK back at the most fun times I spent in advertising, what comes to mind were those years, the 60's and 70's, when I worked at Masius Wynn-Williams with a team of brilliant, dedicated people who loved what they did and were great at it. Joel was one of those people.

We created advertising for brand names like Lego, M&M/Mars, Melitta, Matchbox cars, Baggies plastic bags. We were dedicated, good at what we did and knew it. New business rolled in, we worked 12 hours a day, always pushing the envelope. We were in our stride.

A pushing the envelope moment occurred when Joel and I were frantically getting ready to catch a plane for a client meeting in LA, packing up our presentation for a new campaign we created.

Back then it was not just carrying a laptop or thumb drive containing the presentation. We packed our presentation, illustrated on big cards, in big portfolios, carrying it along with briefcases and suitcases.

With just 45 minutes to get from Manhattan to JFK, usually an hour+ trip, we looked like two cartoon characters rushing up Fifth Avenue to catch a cab. To top things off, it was rush hour, and there were no available cabs in sight.

In panic mode, we rushed over to a car stopped at a red light, knocked on the window, and yelled to the driver, *"Hey mister, how'd you like to make $50?"* Driver: *"How do I do that?"* Us: *"Get us to JFK in 45 minutes."* Driver: *"Jump in."*

$50 was a lot of money in those days.

We made the flight.

It's stories like this, that Joel and I find extraordinarily funny. Donna and Ellen, having heard most of them numerous times, just roll their eyes.

Joel loves Indian food. At the top of the list, Lamb Vindaloo.

LAMB VINDALOO

Joel takes great pleasure in presenting himself as the macho man. So, what better dish for him than Lamb Vindaloo. But, given this recipe is for a broader audience here, it has a little less heat. That said, it's not called *Vindaloo* for nothing.

INGREDIENTS

1 1/2	pounds boned lamb shoulder, cut into 1-inch cubes
1 1/2	teaspoons ground cumin
1	onion, peeled and cut into half rings
6	large cloves of garlic, crushed and peeled
1 1/2	tablespoons Pommery whole-grain mustard
1 1/2	teaspoons ground turmeric
1/2	teaspoon cayenne pepper
2/3	cup vegetable oil
2/3	cup canned coconut milk, stirred to smooth out lumps
2/3	cup of water
1	teaspoon salt
1	teaspoon red wine vinegar
1/4	cup cilantro, chopped

PREP

Combine mustard, turmeric, cayenne, salt and vinegar in a small bowl. Mix well to form a paste.

Preheat oil in a large, nonstick pan. Add onion. Fry until onion is translucent. Add paste mix. Add lamb. Mix well.

Cook 5 minutes, then add coconut milk and 2/3 cup water. Adjust flame, simmer covered for 60 minutes. Lamb should be fork tender in its rich sauce.

Serve lamb over rice. Sprinkle with cilantro.

LOWER EAST SIDE TO THE BERKSHIRES

OUR FRIENDS Larry and Holly are Berkshire locals. Not only are they locals, they come from a long line of Berkshire locals.

As Larry tells it, both his ancestors and Holly's were refugees from Eastern Europe, coming to America in the mid 19th Century, landing on Manhattan's Lower East Side.

In 1891 the Baron de Hirsch Fund was founded in the United States, an offshoot of the Jewish Agricultural and Industrial Aid Society. The fund financed the relocation of Jewish refugees fleeing the pogroms. Many ended up on the Lower East Side. The Fund offered refugees land to farm in the rural Berkshires.

That's how Larry's and Holly's grandparents got to be farmers in a rural Berkshire town. That's how I get first-hand Berkshire history, whenever we meet.

Larry and I take great pleasure in volunteering as chefs, preparing supper for upwards of 130 Berkshire residents. The meals have included BBQ chicken, sausage and pasta, meat loaf—and most recently, a version of Julia Child's beef stew.

It's great fun. We start out a day or two in advance with a visit to Costco. Larry always bumps into someone he knows. Then, chit-chat with the fellow local. Afterwards, Larry gives me chapter and verse on that person—their back stories. It is enough to fill a history book of the Berkshires. After shopping, we meet at the Berkshire Community Center, where supper is prepared. It's heartwarming observing people enjoying the meal we cooked.

NORTH AFRICAN TOMATO SOUP

On a bone chilling winter's day, there's nothing better than this wonderful, rich tomato soup to warm body and spirit.

INGREDIENTS

2	tablespoons olive oil + extra to finish
1	large onion, chopped
1	teaspoon cumin seeds
2	large cloves garlic
3	cups vegetable broth
14	oz. can chopped Italian tomatoes
4	large tomatoes, chopped
1	tablespoon sugar
2	tablespoons chopped cilantro, more to finish
	Salt and fresh ground pepper

PREP

Heat the oil in a pot sufficient in size to hold all ingredients. Add onion, stir until it turns translucent. Add cumin and garlic. Fry on a low flame for 2 minutes.

Pour in stock, both types of tomatoes, sugar, teaspoon of salt and a good grind of pepper. Bring soup to a gentle simmer and cook covered for 20 minutes.

Add cilantro, then blitz using an immersion blender until the tomatoes break down, about a minute. The soup should be thick, add a bit of water if too thick. Serve with a drizzle of olive oil and a sprinkling of cilantro.

MY STUDENT, MY FRIEND

WE MET HUGO when Ellen and I were looking for an apartment to rent in South Beach. He had a lovely place on the bay, available at just the right time and price. We took it.

Five years have past. I have become Hugo's English tutor. He's incredibly diligent and enthusiastic. We connect over FaceTime most weeks. Whether Hugo is in Miami or Columbia, his home country, the connection is easy.

Before deciding he loved Miami, Hugo was the South American heart throb on one of Venezuela's top rated soap operas.

One of the most memorable times we all spent together, was the occasion of Hugo becoming a U.S. Citizen. We celebrated at Carbone in Miami (Hugo pronounces it "Carbone-y").

Ben, Ellen's son, grew up with the restaurant's owners. So, we were treated brilliantly, it was quite the evening. One of those meals you remember for a lifetime.

Tasting several wines, we proceeded to antipasti, octopus, baked clams and beets Siciliana.

Then 2 salads, a Caesar and Caprese.

Then, the pasta, (listed as macaroni on the menu, old school Italian). Linguini Vongole plus a spicy rigatoni in vodka sauce.

OMG, not anymore. But, then came veal parm, salmon oreganata and for Ellen broccoli rabe.

Finally, dessert, cannoli, tartufo, espresso along with a lovely grappa.

What's next? Hugo and I have cooked for each other in Miami, but not yet in the Berkshires. That will happen soon.

I have just the dish to put on the board, one of my favorites, Brandade.

BRANDADE

Talk about bistros and chalkboards, Brandade is one of the ultimate French bistro dishes. Made with salt cod, it harkens back centuries, first introduced into the Southern France gastronomy in the 1700s, when a fish-lover from Nîmes decided to mash a salt cod's flesh with garlic, olive oil and a touch of cream. The inventor deserves France's highest medal, the Legion of Honor.

INGREDIENTS

12	oz salt cod, available in most fish markets with advance order
1	medium russet potato, peeled and cut in quarters
½	cup heavy cream
3	garlic cloves, diced
½	cup good virgin olive oil, some reserved for serving
	Kosher salt
	Good grind of pepper
12	slices of toasted baguette
4	medium sized 3 oz ramekins

Rinse salt cod. Put in a bowl large enough to cover fish with water. Soak for 3 days, changing water twice a day.

After third day, transfer fish to sauté pan, cover with fresh water. Bring water to boil, lower to simmer, cook until cod flakes easily, about 6-7 minutes. Lift fish from pan, transfer to food processor.

While fish is cooking, put the potato in a medium sized pot, cover with water. Bring water to boil, then lower flame to simmer. Cook until potato is tender (about 10 minutes).

Transfer potato to food processor as well.

In a separate small pan bring cream and garlic to boil. Turn off heat, transfer cream, garlic and ¾ of olive oil to food processor bowl.

Add teaspoon salt and several good grinds of pepper to bowl.

Pulse mixture until contents is smooth, about 3 minutes. Beware not to over pulse as contents will turn gummy.

Put oven on broil.

Portion contents equally to ramekins, put small indent in the middle of each portion. Fill indent with remaining olive oil.

Transfer ramekins to broiler. Broil on upper rack until contents are browned, a bit crispy is ok, about 3 minutes. Remove carefully.

Serve individual portions with toasted slices of baguette.

WELCOME PORSCHE OWNERS

MARC IS A BRIT, a brilliant architect, with exquisite taste and a knowing mind to match.

I think of him as one of the gentry in *Downton Abbey*.

Kenny is Marc's husband. Kenny is a gifted copywriter with a charming New Yorker personality who grew up in Brooklyn, reminding me of a young Jewish version of Pete Hamill.

Marc and Kenny enjoy life to its fullest.

Kenny loves elephants so Marc arranged a trip to Kenya to visit an elephant refuge. They traveled first class including staying at a "glam" tent resort, replete with a "proper" chef and a gourmet kitchen.

Marc became infatuated with the giraffes.

After they returned, we invited them to dinner in celebration of a big event. Marc always wanted a Porsche. And now, ordered with special paint, wheels and interior, traveling from Stuttgart, Germany to Newark, New Jersey—the big day arrived!

What better way to celebrate a sexy German sports car than to serve a sexy dish: grilled spare ribs.

GRILLED SPARE RIBS

I love spare ribs, not sure who doesn't. But for Marc & Kenny, true gourmands whose taste buds have been honed from London to Nairobi, these better be good.

INGREDIENTS

(Marinade)

²/₃	cups ketchup
¹/₂	cup vinegar
¹/₄	cup brown sugar
2	teaspoons smoked Spanish paprika
1	teaspoon ground cumin
1	teaspoon Aleppo pepper
1	teaspoon kosher salt
1	teaspoon ground pepper

(Ribs)

2	racks baby back ribs, about 2 ½ pounds. (I prefer Berkshire raised pork or Nieman Ranch brand.)
	Generously sprinkle kosher salt and a few good grinds of black pepper.

PREP

(Marinade)

Combine all ingredients in a sauce pan. Bring to a simmer over medium heat, cook for 5 minutes. The sauce is ready!

(Ribs)

In a large pot, boil enough water to cover the ribs. When water reaches a boil, submerge ribs. Boil ribs over medium flame for 10 minutes.

Remove ribs, drain well and transfer to a large pan. Cover ribs with marinade and refrigerate for 2 hours or overnight. When ready to cook, preheat covered grill (gas or wood fired) to 500°.

Place ribs on grill, adjust temp to 400°. Add ribs and cover. Cook for 5 minutes. Turn, cover with remaining marinade. Close grill and cook for an additional 5 minutes, maintaining temp at 400°. Remove ribs and let rest 10 minutes. There you have it!

MOJITOS IN MIAMI

NOTHING WORKS BETTER than sipping mojitos poolside in Miami, sitting by the bay watching mega million dollar yachts cruise by, the formula for escaping below zero temps and shoveling wet snow in the Northeast.

Enjoying the experience with Regina and Alex, dear pals from the Berkshires, doubles down on the pleasure.

Our friends give meaning to the word, authentic.

Alex worked in family court where he mediated cases concerning child custody, support and divorce. His passion was to protect children caught in the middle between disputing parents to ensure best outcomes for them and their families.

Defining Regina's life's work goes in several directions. Founder of a successful graphic design studio that works 12 hours a day during election seasons creating ads, postcards and flyers to help get responsible people in government. Serving on boards of non-profit organizations supporting causes that make a difference, being a yogi, teaching a practice that elevates mind and body.

Our connection with Regina and Alex speaks to the values we all hold dear, but there's another side. Food!

So whether we're hiking with them at home in the Berks, or sharing mojitos in South Beach, or having a fun weekend in NY munching Via Carota's famous Insalata Verde, our time together always includes eating. (They are Italian of course.)

When they came to our house, knowing Regina has a love affair with vegetables, the chalkboard featured a vegetable tajine.

MOROCCAN VEGETABLE TAJINE

Tajine cooking has a wonderful ability to bring out the flavor and aroma of the food cooked in it. Tajines are common throughout the Middle East and Africa. Made of earthenware they are a great addition to a kitchen. That said, using a pot with a loosely fitted lid is an acceptable option.

INGREDIENTS

1½	cups vegetable broth
⅓	cup olive oil
2	medium onions, chopped
8	garlic cloves, chopped
3	carrots, washed and chopped
2	russet potatoes, peeled and cubed
1	sweet potato, peeled and cubed
1	teaspoon turmeric
1	tablespoon harissa
1	teaspoon ground coriander
1	teaspoon cinnamon
1	tablespoon salt
1	28 oz can whole, peeled tomatoes
½	cup prunes
1	lemon, seeded and juiced
1	cup cilantro
1	cup Italian parsley

PREP

On stovetop, heat oil in a large pot.

Add both kinds of potatoes and onions. Cook on medium flame until lightly browned.

Add garlic, spices and harissa, stir until aromatic, about 3 minutes, continuing on medium flame.

Add carrots, tomatoes, prunes and lemon juice.

Cover pot with lid, leaving it open a bit. Lower flame, simmer for 20-30 minutes, checking partway through to add water or more broth if needed.

Add salt and pepper to taste.

Add cilantro and parsley. Mix just before serving.

Serve with couscous, following package directions.

ELLEN

SHE'S VERY DEFINITIVE

IT WAS OUR first meeting. I clearly remember her arriving at my office for the interview. Ellen was a candidate for City Harvest's Director of Development position. I was on the board's search committee.

I challenged Ellen with a question. "If you were asked to select among being CH's head of fundraising, or marketing, or PR, which would you choose?"

Her definitive response, "None, I'd need to do all three."

That clinched it for me, Ellen was hired.

After a decade of service, I revolved off CH's board. One day I ran into Ellen on the street. We spent a few minutes catching up, then I asked her out for dinner. Another definitive answer came forth, "How about lunch?"

Applying all the charm I could muster, she ultimately agreed to dinner, not an easy sell.

One date led to another, then another. I invited Ellen out to a house I was renting in Sag Harbor, suggesting lobster for dinner. To my amazement she agreed.

Dinnertime arrived. I began boiling water. Ellen, "What's that for?" Me, "The lobsters". Ellen, "Oh no. You can't do that." So, we walked the lobsters down to the bay and watched them swim off.

Now, nineteen years later, and after many dinners (never again lobster), her favorite dish is a plate of my grilled peppers, baked cipollini onions, and broccoli rabe sauteed in garlic.

Ellen's very definitive. Guess that's why I love her so much. This time she's served soup.

ZA'ATAR AND ALEPPO SPICED BUTTERNUT SQUASH, SWEET POTATO, CARROT SOUP

Ellen loves soup, she also loves squash, sweet potatoes and carrots.

I know she's definitive, so how could I go wrong?

INGREDIENTS

1	butternut squash, peeled and diced
2	carrots, peeled and diced
1	large sweet potatoe, peeled and diced
¼	cup olive oil
1	teaspoon ground cumin
5	cups vegetable broth
4	tablespoons za'atar, plus extra for garnish
½	teaspoon Aleppo pepper

PREP

Preheat oven to 350°. Put squash, sweet potato and carrots in a large bowl, toss with olive oil, cumin and 1 teaspoon pepper.

Spread veggies onto a baking sheet in a single layer, roast for 35 minutes or until fork-tender. Transfer to a large pot, add vegetable broth, cook over low heat for 20 minutes. Use an immersion blender to puree until smooth and creamy in consistency.

Serve hot, adding more za'atar, salt and pepper to taste.

EPILOGUE

Thirty groups of friends, thirty stories, thirty recipes. These and a bunch more (that came before I found my chalkboard) are the ingredients, sweet and savory, salty and spicy, haphazardly added to the pot, that cooked up my life.

More to the larder? Perhaps.

Neil Fox
Spring 2023

P.S. I've come to realize that my chalkboard has magical qualities. Guests can't help smiling, feeling special and cared for when they enter our kitchen and discover the chalkboard prepared just for them.

The feeling of pleasure goes two ways, for them and me.

So, consider acquiring a chalkboard and a box of chalk. Partake in the joyful experience, creating and knowing, *What's on the Board.*

ACKNOWLEDGEMENTS

Mindy and Jason, my children. More than family, they are my most cherished friends and advisors. My greatest of life's gifts. My teachers.

Ellen, my love, my muse, my source of inspiration. After working together for five years, I asked her to dinner. Now, 19 years later our life is characterized each day with laughter. I'm a lucky man.

Nan is an artist whose work gives meaning to the word, art. Her expressions of encouragement have been the fuel that have brought this book to life.

One of the great pleasures in creating this book has been working with Mike Grinley. Mike is an accomplished art director and designer. He and I collaborated on my first book, *The Roots of it All*. Mike's creative eye, ability to bring to life the tone and manner of what I wanted to capture has been a fun fest from start to finish. What's left? Mike and his wife coming by to see *What's on the Board?*, just for them.